BIG
Bear Feet

Cover Illustration by Margarita Sikorskaia

Softcover ISBN 13: 978-1-7327646-0-6
Hardcover ISBN 13: 978-1-7346743-0-9

Printed in the United States of America

Cover and interior design by James Monroe Design, LLC.

Lucky Luke, LLC.
4335 Matthew Court
Eagan, Minnesota 55123

www.KevinLovegreen.com
Quantity discounts available!

Chapter 1

The sun is going down so fast that I can almost see it moving through the trees. Deep-red clouds streak across a purplish-blue sky. I can't help but smile as I picture Grandpa saying, "A red sky at night is a sailor's delight." That means tomorrow will be another amazing fall day in Minnesota. The woods glow as if the leaves were millions of gold coins shimmering from the trees.

The color reminds me of an ancient Egyptian tomb loaded with gold to honor a great king. For a moment, I imagine I'm an explorer entering a giant burial room. I need to cover my eyes as the sunrays shine down through the cracks in the ceiling.

But then my eyes pop open as Dad taps on my leg. I'm instantly transported back to reality. I remember I'm sitting in a tree stand with my dad and my sister, Crystal, at our hunting land. My dad is one of the greatest hunters I know and loves bringing us along to show us the ropes. Our goal this weekend is to get Crystal her first bear. I guess the boys at school don't believe she has the guts to shoot one. She's determined to prove them wrong.

I'm Luke. If you know me, you know I love to hunt—and black bears are really exciting to go after. Even though I'm not old enough to hunt bears myself, I have sat with Dad several times over the last two years while he's hunted them. Crystal is older than me, so she's lucky enough to be the hunter this year. Dad and I are rooting for her. But I also know the time is coming for me to be in the hot seat. Next year is my year. I can't wait!

Without lifting his hand, Dad points into the woods, past the bait barrel. In Minnesota, bear season is in the fall. And the best way to hunt bears is to load up a bait station. A bait station is basically a big barrel full of food bears like to eat. Things such as bread, doughnuts, and cookies work great. The goal is to get them hitting the bait a couple of weeks before the actual hunting begins. Then when the season starts, we sneak to our stands and hope a bear will come to the bait station during daylight.

It sounds like a simple plan. But let me tell you, it's not all that easy to trick a big bear. Thanks to the trail cameras pointing at the bait, we have seen pictures of several good-sized bears hitting the food lately. Yet we've been sitting in the stand for hours, and we're still waiting for our first bear to show.

Dad points again to the bait barrel. I look out, then do a double take. I see a black streak, but I don't really understand what I'm looking at.

I glance over at Crystal for some confirmation. Clearly, she knows what it is. Her eyes show a cross between fear and excitement.

I know not to make any noise at this point—Dad has taught me well. So I silently mouth, "A bear?" to Crystal.

She nods up and down so slowly that the red ponytail poking out of her hat hardly moves. Also in slow motion, I turn back to the bait station. This time, I can tell it's a bear. Or at least I can tell it's the top of his back. The pure black fur is unmistakable. It sticks out against the thick green brush.

Clearly in no hurry, he heads toward us and the bait barrel. He never makes a sound— not one broken branch. Soon he'll be out in the open, and Crystal can take her shot.

This is it! I'm so excited for Crystal. We've sat in the stand for so many hours without seeing or hearing anything that resembles a bear. But now Crystal will finally get to shoot a bear for the first time. My heart pounds, and my hands shake in my lap as I wait for the bear to step out.

But then the bear stops. Suddenly, the black fur disappears. Silence! I give Dad a puzzled look.

Dad bends over so he can whisper into my ear. "He lay down."

Crystal gives me the same puzzled expression. I show her the "down" signal we use with our dog, Trigger. She understands.

I turn back to where I last spotted the bear. I can now see flies or mosquitoes or both hovering around. That's a sure sign the bear is still there. But without seeing him, I have no idea what his next move will be.

Helplessly, we sit in the stand, hoping he'll get up and make the last few steps to the bait barrel. But with each passing minute, the light gets squeezed out of the woods. As our shooting time runs out, my heart sinks— but probably not as much as Crystal's.

"He's not coming in," Dad whispers. "He knows we're here."

"Now what?" I whisper back.

"We need to climb down and sneak out of here," Dad says loudly enough for both Crystal and me to hear.

Crystal's eyes get big again. "I am not getting down with that bear right over there," she says, trying to contain the sound to our stand.

"Okay," Dad whispers with a smirk. "You can stay here tonight. We'll come and get you tomorrow."

Crystal just cocks her head and gives Dad "the look."

"Follow me," Dad says. "We'll be fine."

Dad climbs down. I'm right behind him, and Crystal doesn't waste any time either. As soon as my foot hits the ground, the feeling of safety vanishes. We are now on the ground—just like the bear! Quickly, we hurry down the trail and get out of there without any issues.

Unfortunately, there's no luck for Crystal this season. But I already can't wait to see what happens next year.

Chapter 2

A year flies by. It's now another steamy day in August. I'm lying on my bedroom floor, enjoying the air conditioning and picking off the endless zombies in my video game. I hear my dad whistle for me.

"Give me a minute!" I shout.

I crush through the last slow-walking creepers and make it to a level I have never reached before.

"Yes!" I exclaim.

Quickly, I pause the game, then race down the stairs.

"What's up, Dad?" I ask.

"It's time to run to the bakery to see what they have left over from the weekend," Dad says. He smiles and rubs his hands together, as if we were about to pick up the mother lode of something really good.

I shake my head. "Oh boy," I say with hesitation.

That's my typical response when Dad's either trying to be funny or trying to get me excited to do something that will take a lot of work. This time, he's trying to be funny.

We're off to the local bakery to pick up some leftover bread and buns. In a way, this is the "hunt" before the hunt. You see, bear season is just around the corner. That means we have to start filling our chest freezer with any and all bread, pastries, and other sweets. Then right before the season begins, we'll bring our goodies up to the hunting land to set up the bait stations.

We pull up to the bakery, jump out of the Suburban, and head into the store.

"How's it going today?" Dad asks the young guy standing behind the counter and wearing a white bib chock-full of flour.

"Pretty good. What can I help you with?" the young guy says politely.

"I'm wondering what you have left over that we can take off your hands. We use it to feed bears," Dad adds quietly enough so the two people shopping an aisle over don't hear.

With a quick smile, the guy says, "Ah, that's what you're here for. Drive around to the back door. I'll meet you there. I think you'll like what we have today."

"Sounds good!" Dad replies.

With a zip in his step, Dad heads for the parking lot. I have to turn it up a notch to keep pace. In a short time, we're parked in back. The young guy appears with four huge plastic bags full of individually wrapped bread loaves. There must be at least fifteen loaves in each bag.

"Sweet!" I say, heaving the bags into the back of our Suburban.

On our way home, Dad quickly calls his buddy Greg to let him know the good news. Greg's daughter, Megan, is Crystal's best friend. My dad invited Greg up for a bear hunt a couple of years ago. He had so much fun, he has turned into a bear-hunting machine ever since. Megan hunts too.

"We just picked up the mother lode of bread from the bakery. My whole back is filled," Dad says into the speaker.

"Nice work!" Greg replies. "I picked up four barrels last night from the bait shop up north. I got a barrel each of Peeps, chocolate chip cookies, red licorice, and peanut M&Ms!" he adds with the excitement of a little kid.

My dad and Greg are really funny when it comes to getting bait. It's a friendly competition of who can find the best stuff.

"You're hilarious," Dad says. "Well, the bears will be happy this year. I just hope we can keep you out of the cookie barrel," he jokes.

"Yah, yah," Greg says with a laugh.

Chapter 3

The days fly by. Before I know it, it's the last Saturday in August. Dad, Crystal, and I are heading over to pick up Greg and Megan. It's time to head to the hunting cabin. We have a few things to prep for bear season, which starts next weekend.

When we pull up, Greg is standing in front of his trailer. It's quite a sight to see. It's plumb-full with a four-wheeler, a little plastic trailer, and four fifty-five-gallon black barrels. Greg's arms are crossed as if he were mad or as if he were guarding his trailer. He has the body of an offensive lineman, and he's wearing his matching camo hat and jacket. He looks like a force to be reckoned with. Actually, he's a funny guy who likes to do a lot of harassing.

"Howdy, boys—and Crystal! I was wondering if you'd ever get here," Greg says in his typical joking fashion.

Despite the jokes, there's no time for messing around. Right away, we hook up the trailer and throw Greg and Megan's gear in the Suburban. Then we're off for the two-hour drive north to our hunting cabin.

It's still early when we pull up to the gate that leads to the place I love to be. The warm air hits me when I jump out. It isn't super-August-hot yet, but you can tell the day's heat is just getting started.

After unloading, first on our to-do list is setting up the bait stations. Megan hooks their trailer to their four-wheeler. Crystal does the same with our trailer and four-wheeler from the garage. We quickly fill our trailer full of the bread loaves we got from the bakery.

Using a giant screwdriver, Greg wedges the tops off the barrels he brought. The smell of chocolate chip cookies and other sweets fills the air. My mouth starts watering.

"Remember not to eat any of this stuff," Dad says, seeing my reaction. "It all came from the floor of the factory. Most of it is expired. That's why they sell it for bear bait."

"That's not fair!" Megan shoots back. "It's making me really hungry."

Apparently, I'm not the only one whose mouth is watering.

We fill the goodies from the big barrels into white five-gallon buckets. Next, Greg sets in two gallons of maple syrup.

"The icing on the cake," he says with a big smile.

We then finish things off by jamming a bunch of bread loaves in every open spot we can find. Finally, one big bag of corn goes on top, to hold everything in place. The trailers are now stacked full of bait. I wouldn't be surprised if we had bears following behind us, picking up scraps that fell off.

With ease, Dad slides on our four-wheeler behind Crystal. Then we all watch in amusement as Greg tries to get on their four-wheeler behind Megan. He maneuvers his giant leg over the seat, smooshes Megan forward, and rolls into position with a steady groan.

"I'm on!" Greg yells. He raises both arms as if indicating a touchdown.

"Oh my goodness," Megan says as she straightens herself back up. She swipes her midlength brown hair from out of her eyes and readjusts her ball cap.

After a good chuckle, we're ready to cruise to our stands. Me, I hop on my little red four-wheeler as if it were a horse waiting for action. I love riding solo. Driving a four-wheeler is one of my favorite things to do at the cabin. I could race around on this sweet machine for hours.

Our hunting land is full of off-white poplar trees. Some big brown oaks are also scattered about. The trails cut through the trees and wind around the property. Our two bear stands are tucked deep in the swampiest part of the land. These are areas we can hardly walk through because of all the water, tall grass, and thick brush. Bears like to hide in the thick stuff, where people typically won't see them. Also, it's not as hot in there because the sunlight can't get through. The stands are on separate corners of the land, so there's some distance between them.

After several minutes of bouncing down the trail, we make the final turn. We carefully ease through the woods on the cutoff trail that takes us to a waiting fifty-five-gallon barrel near our stand. The bait station has been here for years, so not much grass grows around the barrel.

As we turn off the four-wheelers, silence settles back into the woods. It gets a little scary. A bear could easily be lying in the tall grass just out of sight. But I guess I'm not too worried. We're all here together. No bear in its right mind would want anything to do with a group of people. Even so, I still keep a watchful eye out. Just like the Secret Service, I'm always on guard at the bait site.

"Okay, it's time to load this barrel up. Let's give them something they can't resist," Greg says, taking charge. "Megan, bring me the bucket of M&Ms. That goes in first. And Luke, grab me the bucket of cookies. No nibbling!" he orders like a field sergeant.

"Yes, sir!" I bark back, playing along.

"Crystal, you're next," Greg says. "Bring me the yellow Peeps, or something else good to eat."

We hand one bucket after the next to Greg. He pours the contents into the bait barrel as if creating a magic potion. When the barrel is almost full, he raises his hand.

"Yes, Greg? Do you have a question?" Dad asks like a sarcastic teacher.

"Funny," Greg zings back. "But no, I don't have a question. I have something to say: THE BARREL IS READY!" he loudly announces to the woods.

Then he looks at Crystal, Megan, and me with a big satisfied smile.

"You have to let the bears know, you know," he explains.

We all shake our heads.

Megan lets out her typical response: "Oh my. You're so weird."

"I'm not done yet," Greg says like a mad scientist. "Stand back—I don't want anyone to get hurt."

He gets behind the barrel and carefully pushes it over. When it crashes to the ground, a little bit of everything spills out.

"Perfect! Just enough to tease them," Dad says. "Now, open up a few more loaves of bread. Let's scatter them around the opening of the barrel."

We kids each open four bagged loaves. The bread slides out of each bag in one piece, like a big Tootsie Roll. I make the perfect *plop* sound when mine hits the ground.

"Gross!" both girls say together.

That gets a chuckle out of Greg. He winks at me as he pulls out the syrup.

"Almost the final touch," he says.

He oozes the sweet-smelling syrup all over the bread. He's careful not to get any syrup on his rubber boots, but now I remember why he wears them.

He then grabs a plastic spray bottle from the trailer. With a funny grin, he bounces to the tree behind the barrel. He bobs his head up and down all the way there, as if he were dancing to a good song.

"A new secret weapon I read about," he says.

Greg sprays a long stream of the liquid on the tree and way up in the branches. An amazing smell overtakes us. It's sweet and smoky. It reminds me of a BBQ restaurant.

"What do you have there?" Dad asks.

"This is liquid smoke and a sweet oil mixed with water. That smell will travel all over the woods and drive those bears crazy," Greg says. "The guy at the bait shop told me he's been doing it for years. I figure we have nothing to lose."

"You're funny," Dad says, smiling as usual. He seems to be getting a kick out of Greg's determination to get a bear to hit the bait.

Next, Greg brings out a gallon of used french fry oil he got from a restaurant. He pours it on the ground in front of the bread and Peeps.

"Do you remember why we do this?" he asks me.

"Yep. We want the bears to get it on their feet and track it through the woods. That way, the other bears can follow the scent back to the bait."

"Bingo!" Greg says. "And now we are done here. Load up! We're off to the next spot."

"Whoa, whoa, whoa," Dad says. "You forgot one very important thing."

Dad pulls a trail camera from the pouch on the back of our four-wheeler.

"Oh man. I'm glad you remembered that," Greg says.

Trail cameras are really cool. They take digital photos whenever movement triggers them. Our goal is to get pictures of bears hitting the bait. Checking the photos is nearly as exciting as hunting. The time-stamped shots give us all kinds of information: how long it takes a bear to find the bait, what time of day bears hit the bait, how big the bears are, and so on. We've gotten a bunch of really fun photos in the past. This year should be no different.

Dad fastens the camera to a tree five steps in front of the bait. We make sure there's no grass or weeds in front of the camera. Otherwise, that might trigger it to take photos of nothing.

After a team high five, we load up and make the five-minute ride over to Megan and Greg's spot. Their stand is on the edge of a swamp in a little field opening. They have a bait barrel set up there too. The grass is chest-high in this area. So the weekend before, Dad used the tractor and brush mower to cut a trail to the site. He then mowed a big circle around the barrel.

Once again, Greg immediately dives into action. He directs us to prepare the bait station just as we did at our site. In about a half hour, the barrel and trail camera are ready. And then we're off, heading back to the cabin.

The next thing on our to-do list is really fun. We get to do some target practice at our safe shooting area on the property. It's partly to make sure our guns are sighted in properly and partly to make sure our aim is good. Either way, it's a blast!

Down our shooting lane, we have a piece of plywood propped up at fifty yards and another at twenty-five yards. We staple three targets to each. Megan and Crystal both shoot Remington .243 rifles with scopes. They're great shots. They should be—they've been practicing together for a couple of years. This will be Crystal's and Megan's second year hunting bears. The bears have no chance against the girls. All Megan and Crystal need is to see one during shooting light.

I love shooting my Remington 20-gauge shotgun with a slug. I don't have a scope. I like the challenge of shooting with an open sight. Our bear bait is only twenty-five steps from our stand, and I'm deadly at that close distance. I'm confident that when my big lead slug hits a bear, it will put him down.

I'm finally old enough this year to hunt bears. I can't wait for my turn. Crystal will get the first shot, and I'm okay with that. She has been trying really hard to get one. It would be so cool to see her get her first bear. But rest assured, when the time comes for me to be in the hot seat, I'll be ready!

We each take six careful shots. The dads are impressed because all the shots are close enough to the bull's-eye to kill a bear. Satisfied, we clean our guns and put them back in their cases. We're confident and excited to put our practice to work when the season starts next weekend.

Chapter 4

It's Friday evening, the night before hunting begins, and we're pulling through the cabin gate. Greg and Megan follow close behind us. The sun is just going down. The magical pink, red, and blue colors are amazing as they streak through the sky.

I have a new skip in my step as I bound out of the Suburban. In a surprising change of plans, Crystal decided to miss opening weekend. Instead, she'll be volunteering with Mom to cook at a homeless shelter. It counts toward her school service hours.

She's clearly a little bummed out about missing the weekend, but she knows she's doing a good deed by volunteering. And there will be other bear-hunting weekends. The season lasts for about six weeks.

I feel bad for Crystal . . . but I feel really excited for myself! I'm in the hot seat now, and I'll finally have a chance to get my first bear.

Crystal seems happy for me too. But the way she fired Megan up before we left, I think maybe she's rooting more for Megan than for me! I'm okay either way.

But for right now, I'm going to get the car unloaded in record time. I have a plan of action.

"Hey, Dad," I say once the last bag is tossed inside. "Can Megan and I run out and grab the memory cards from the trail cameras?"

My dad looks at Greg. "What do you think? Can we trust them to swap out the cards and get back here without getting eaten?" He's holding back a smirk.

"Luke, are you wearing your steel underwear?" Greg asks, trying to seem very serious. "You'll need them if a bear comes after you." He uses his hands to mimic bear jaws clamping down on me.

"Nah, I don't need them. I just need to outrun Megan, right?" I reply, feeling good about my quick response.

"Good luck with that," Megan jumps in. "I'm the second-fastest on my softball team. You're going to be the bear snack, not me."

Dad laughs, then nods toward the four-wheelers. "Okay. You guys go ahead and get the memory cards. Just remember to keep the four-wheelers running. No bear will bother you with the engines running."

Greg gives me two new memory cards to replace the ones we'll bring back. I slide them carefully in my front left pocket. Then Megan and I are out the door in a flash.

It's almost dark now, so I take it easy as I lead the way with my little red four-wheeler. When we drive past one of our small fields, we see three deer on alert. They watch us closely for a couple of seconds, then they bolt across the field and leap into the woods.

I give Megan a thumbs-up. It's always fun to see deer on our property.

We make the turn toward Megan's bait barrel. My heart starts to race. I grip the four-wheeler handles a little tighter. I'm just not sure what we'll see when the headlights hit the barrel. For all we know, a bear could be munching on Peeps right now!

I slow to a halt and let the bouncing headlight settle on the barrel. To my surprise, it's been spun around and moved about five feet into the woods. A bear is the only animal big enough to move that barrel. I wonder where the bear is now.

As if I just arrived at a crime scene, my eyes grow wide and quickly scan back and forth for anything black. Sensing the coast is clear, I drive right up next to the camera.

From the safety of my running four-wheeler, I reach over, open the camera, and slide out the precious memory card. Treating it as if it contained top-secret Russian information, I carefully slide the card into my right pocket. I then insert the new card.

This mission is almost complete. Now we just have to get out of here.

But then I turn to the barrel one more time. I carefully analyze the area again, hoping to find more clues. Because the barrel faces away from me, I can't tell how much of the bait has been eaten. Curiosity is killing me. I have to do it. I have to turn the barrel around. But that means I have to get off my four-wheeler!

I slide off my seat and ease toward the barrel. I leave the four-wheeler running, as Dad instructed. But then an uneasy feeling hits me. If a twig were to snap, I wouldn't be able to hear it over the motor. In other words, if a bear were to step out of the woods, I wouldn't have a clue!

"What are you doing, you goof?" Megan says loudly, over the motor noise.

I quickly pat the air with both hands, signaling her to be quiet. We really shouldn't make that much noise. Sounds from a four-wheeler will keep a bear away from the bait station for a while. But sounds from a human could scare it off for good. Since we're hunting tomorrow, we don't want that.

As Megan puts her hand over her mouth, realizing she was too loud, I refocus on my mission. I creep closer, grab the barrel with my left hand, and spin it around.

Suddenly, there's a flash of movement! I gasp and jump back, scared to death.

It takes me a second to realize it's not a bear but a small, skinny tree. Apparently, the tree had gotten bent and trapped under the barrel. When I moved the barrel, I freed the tree to spring back up.

I can hear Megan laughing at me through her cupped hand. I turn to her and shake my head in relief, glad it's only a tree and I'm still alive.

Taking a quick deep breath, I return to the barrel and pull it back to its original spot. With Megan's headlight shining inside, I can now see it's half empty. The bears have definitely been hitting it, which is great news!

I race back to my waiting four-wheeler. For my own safety, I'm ready to get out of here. Plus, spreading human scent at a bait area isn't a good idea. A bear has one of the best noses of any animal. They might not return to this all-you-can-eat buffet if they pick up human scent.

Megan and I cruise out of there and make our way over to the bait barrel near my stand. I'm so excited. I can't wait to see if my bait has been hit as hard as Megan's.

Our headlights shine on the barrel. Instantly, I feel like a deflated balloon. It doesn't look like the bait has been hit at all. Still, nothing will stop me from being in that stand tomorrow. As long as you put in your time, anything can happen when it comes to hunting.

Without messing around, I swap the memory card in the camera, then lead the way back to the cabin. When we get close enough to see the glow of the cabin lights, I feel a little relief. I admit it's a little spooky driving on the trails at night, knowing there are bears around!

And now comes the fun part—checking out the photos on the memory cards. Who knows what we'll see!

Chapter 5

Inside the cabin, the first thing we do is grab Dad's laptop. We head into the kitchen so everyone can gather round to see the photos.

The kitchen is the coolest place in our cabin. The ceiling is raised up high, and there are a bunch of awesome animals mounted on the walls and above the cupboards.

There is the giant elk Dad got last year in Colorado with his bow. That big dude overlooks the whole kitchen.

Then there are the five biggest bucks that have been taken from our property. They are proudly displayed on the wall facing the living room, for all to see.

Over the stove, there's a bobcat reaching for my first turkey. The turkey is mounted with his wings wide open, as if he were trying to fly away. Every time I look up at that turkey, it brings me back to that amazing day when Dad took me out on my first turkey hunt.

Next to them, proudly coming out of the corner, is a full-mounted coyote with a deer leg in its mouth. It was the first coyote Dad ever shot. It's a cool reminder that those guys are running all around here.

There are other things on the walls too, such as a mule deer from Alberta and a bunch of deer racks from our old cabin. As I said, I think this is one of the coolest places ever.

I turn my focus back to the laptop when I hear Megan boot it up. She slides in the first memory card, the one from her stand.

"Three hundred and twenty-four pictures!" I announce.

"Nice," Greg pipes in. "Open those babies up. Let's see what we have."

I double-click the first photo. It opens to fill the whole screen.

"Oh, that's a scary one!" Greg yells out.

Dad is in the living room, but Greg's yell gets his attention. Dad quickly scoots over to take a look at the screen.

We all laugh because it's a way-too-close-up shot of Dad's face as he was attaching the camera to the tree.

"Watch out for that one eating your cookies," Dad says to Megan.

After another laugh, we quickly move on to the next photos. There are a couple of crows, which are usually the first to find the bait. Then we all cheer in unison when the first shot of a medium-sized black bear pops up.

"What time?" Dad asks.

I look at the time stamp on the bottom of the picture. "Eleven forty-five p.m. on Tuesday."

"Interesting," Megan says. "It took him four days to find it."

"Yah, but now watch. I bet he didn't leave it," Greg says, knowing he filled the bait station with goodies bears love.

Sure enough, there are about forty pictures of the bear that night. The camera is set for a one-minute delay before it takes another picture. So that means the bear hung around for about forty-five minutes.

Then the photos show that he returned the next night around midnight. We scroll through shots of him sitting, standing, and even lying down by the barrel. It's cool watching time play out.

But when the next photo pops up, we all suddenly take in a deep breath. There's a giant bear butt taking up the whole screen.

In the next picture, the bear is standing broadside, so we can see just how big he is.

"Oh my goodness—he's huge!" Megan yells with eyes popped wide open.

"Now, *that's* what we're looking for!" Greg says. He crowds in to take a good look. "It says he arrived at two twenty-six on Thursday morning."

There's no quick scrolling now. I slow down so we can stare at each picture. We're like a group of doctors looking at a really exciting batch of x-rays.

"What do you think that guy weighs?" I ask the group.

"I don't know. What do you think?" Greg says, looking at my dad, who has seen the most bears.

"Hmm . . ." Dad says through tight lips and a half smile. "Considering how big he is compared to the barrel, he must be around four hundred pounds."

"Oh—my—goodness!" Megan says, drawing out each word. "That's kinda scary, actually. Something that big is out there!" She crouches back in her chair.

"Don't you worry, my little Megan—I'll be right there to protect you!" Greg says with his typical sarcasm as he wraps her in his arms.

"Yeah, but who'll be there to protect you?" Dad says, crinkling his forehead at Greg.

Greg puts his hand to his chin. "That's a good question."

I continue to click through the final pictures. Soon we're looking at photos from earlier today. At 5:37 p.m., the big guy was back again. It's a great sign—that's prime shooting time. If he sticks to the same pattern tomorrow, Megan will have a shot at him!

I click through about sixty pictures of him hanging around the bait for about an hour. The next photos show that he returned to the bait station at 8:16 p.m. It gets me thinking.

"Megan, what time did we get to your stand tonight?" I ask like Sherlock Holmes following a lead.

"I don't know," she says with a shrug. "But it was pretty dark."

I click on a photo from 8:22. The bear is looking up, as if he's heard something. The very next picture is me sitting on the four-wheeler. It's from 8:23—only one minute later!

I slowly turn toward Megan. Her head is tilted down, and an "Are you kidding me?" look is written all over her face.

"Oh my goodness!" she barks out.

"We scared him off the bait!" I say, shaking my head. "And the barrel—check it out!" I click back to the previous photo. "Here, the barrel opening is facing the camera. But it was facing backward when we found it. He must have kicked it when he ran away."

"And you went over there and pulled it back in place, you nut!" Megan crouches back once again. This time, she also covers her face, as if hiding from the image of me getting eaten by the bear.

"Well, it's a good thing his mouth was full of chocolate chip cookies. That way, he didn't have to bother with your leg," Greg says, keeping a straight face.

"Dad, that's not funny at all!" Megan says.

My dad laughs and shakes his head. "Honestly, he wasn't going to bother you, Luke. Bears don't want anything to do with us. I'm sure he was just disappointed that you interrupted his dinner. Let's just hope he didn't go far. We want him to come back tomorrow so Megan can show him who's the boss."

We've finished all the photos on that memory card, so I trade it for the card from our stand. Unfortunately, the action at our stand was not nearly as exciting as it was at Megan's.

The first bear didn't hit the bait until Thursday. It was only a small bear, though. There are a few shots of other small bears— nothing big enough to shoot. And on top of it, no bears came to the bait during shooting light.

The coolest photos, I guess, are of a sow—a female bear—and her two small cubs. Megan does a lot of oohing and aahing. Even I have to admit the little ones are very cute. The sow is big, but it's illegal to shoot a mom with cubs. We would never even think about it, anyway.

"Well, those shots were a little disappointing," I say, closing up the laptop. "But it's not going to stop me from putting some time in on the stand. You never know when a bear might show up or what else you get to see."

"That's the right attitude," Dad replies. "We all know there's a lot more to hunting than shooting an animal."

Dad is right. I remember one weekend during deer season, we spent hours in the stand without seeing a deer, yet I didn't get bored. That's because I made friends with a red squirrel that kept sneaking up our tree to check us out. And then I counted five different types of birds. I saw chickadees, blue jays, a cardinal, a grouse, plus a red-tailed hawk that glided over us. As if that weren't cool enough, we even had a skunk mosey on by us. I simply love spending time in the woods.

So whatever tomorrow brings, I'll be ready!

Chapter 6

Opening day finally comes! It's a long day for me. Typically, bears hit the bait around dusk, which comes around 7:30 p.m. this time of the year. So we plan to head to our stands around 4:00 p.m. That means I have to wait nearly all day—and it's killing me!

After hours of waiting, Dad finally says it's time to get a bite to eat before we head out. My adrenaline kicks in. Megan and I look at each other, high-five, and race into the kitchen.

After a quick turkey sandwich with extra mayo, I scoot to the mudroom. I dig for my camo clothes in my duffel bag. It's pretty warm out, so I figure my long-sleeve shirt will be enough. But I still grab my light jacket just in case it cools down at dark.

Next, I go to the big green gun safe, which Dad has already opened. My trusty 20-gauge shotgun is standing at attention, right next to my grandpa's old .22 rifle. I pull out my shotgun, then quickly look on top of the safe for my box of slugs. Bingo! I pull five slugs from the box.

"Are you ready to go, Dad?" I ask as I make my way through the mudroom.

"Yes, sir, Lucky Luke. Let's make this happen."

Dad and I head for the door. We stop by Megan, who's sitting on the bench, tying her boots.

"Good luck, Ms. Megan," Dad says. "I hope you get to see that giant."

"Thanks. I hope I see him too!" Megan replies. "And good luck to you, Luke!"

Greg comes into the room, clapping his hands together. "Come on, come on, come on! They're beating us out!"

"Hold your horses! I'm almost ready. Could you at least get my gun?" Megan asks her dad in a voice as if she were overworked.

"It's already on the four-wheeler," Greg says. "Is there anything else your personal attendant and guide can do for you?" He stands at attention with his arms tight to his sides.

"Good luck with that," Dad whispers to Megan, pointing at Greg. He smirks as we walk out the door.

I slip my gun into the old brown canvas case lying on the table in the garage. Then we hop on the four-wheeler. Dad drives, and I ride on the back with my gun cradled between us. Off we head!

After the first turn, Dad eases to a crawl. I peek over his shoulder to see what's going on. I spot a ruffed grouse standing proud right in the middle of the road. As we move closer, the bird clearly decides he's had enough of us. He puts his head down and runs into the woods. When we pull up to the spot where he entered the woods, I can see him sneaking through the grass.

"That's cool," I say.

"Yep," Dad replies.

As we head down the road, I scan like a hawk, trying to spot another critter of some sort. The woods are pretty thick and green, so I have a hard time seeing anything. In the distance, I do spot a porcupine up in an oak tree.

We approach our familiar parking spot near the trail leading to the stand. Dad shuts off the engine. The immediate silence is calming.

I unzip my gun case and pull out my trusty 20-gauge. It sends a charge of energy through my body. First things first, I make sure the safety is on.

This is it. It's "go time," as Dad always says. There just isn't anything like the feeling of the first day of a hunt. We've been waiting a long time for this moment. Duck season, deer season, turkey season, or bear season—the opening day excitement is all the same to me. I simply can't wait to see how it'll play out.

I dig into my pocket and feel the familiar cold brass ring of one of the slugs. I drop it in the chamber, then I jam the pump forward with authority. And just like that, I'm locked and loaded. I slide two more shells into the bottom chamber and give Dad a crisp thumbs-up.

"Safety on?" Dad asks.

"Yep."

"Let's do this," he says. He grabs the backpack, then gestures to me. "You better lead the way—you have the gun."

Being in front is a pretty cool feeling. Like a safari guide in the jungles of Africa, I creep forward, keeping a close eye out for danger. Everything is good until I catch sight of the trail that leads to our stand. Then it hits me: we are really close to the bait. A bear could easily be standing there right now! I grip my gun a little tighter, and all my senses are alive. I slow my pace, scanning carefully as we ease toward the stand.

We come up to an open patch of semidried mud on the trail. To my surprise, there are two giant bear tracks smack-dab in the middle.

"Those are some big bear feet," Dad whispers.

With wildly surprised eyes, I nod. "That could be the giant we saw on the trail camera," I quietly say back.

"Or another one. Who knows?" Dad says optimistically.

I throw my glove down and snap a picture with my phone to show Megan later.

That track could have been made two days ago or two minutes ago. I'm not skilled enough to know. But it's just another reminder that a bear—a giant bear—could be just feet away right now!

I try desperately to make it to the stand undetected. But the small dead branches under the grass make silent walking almost impossible. Tension builds as we slink forward. Now, the stand is in my sights. I still can't see the bait, though. With each step, I squeeze my eyes with laser-like focus. I try to detect any glimpse of black hair between the small openings in the thick brush. Nothing.

Suddenly, I feel Dad tap me on my shoulder. Snapping my focus, I spring my head around, wondering if he sees something. Instead, he points to my gun and gives me a nod. Without any words, I understand. I pass him my gun so I can safely climb up into the stand.

As I head up the fourteen-foot steel ladder, I stop each time the metal creaks. I hope the foreign sound won't make its way through the woods and scare any nearby bear away.

I keep peeking over my left shoulder as I climb, trying to see the bait barrel. Finally, I can see it. I freeze for a second. Like an owl, I crank my head as far as I can, then I pan the area from left to right, and then again from right to left. I look for anything black or moving. I spot nothing out of the ordinary. I negotiate the last two steps, then settle myself into the bench seat.

Hand over fist, Dad climbs up and slides in next to me. He situates the backpack under the bench, slips my gun off his shoulder, and passes it to me.

With my trusty gun in my hands, I draw in a long, deep breath. I let it out slowly as my back sinks into the seat. Now we wait!

Chapter 7

Like a lion, I scan the forest around us. My eyes settle in on the black barrel. I'm trying to see if any bait has been eaten since the trail camera pictures from last night. From the looks of it, I'm not convinced a bear has visited the barrel today.

I'm a little disappointed, but I have to set that aside. Just because a bear hasn't been here yet doesn't mean one won't walk in at any minute. We just need to wait and see. My dad and grandpa have been telling me this since I was a little kid. I can picture Grandpa saying, "Luke, patience is a hunter's best friend." Sometimes it's hard to be patient and stay put in a stand. There's no question that I prefer action!

As I focus harder on the barrel, I can see movement. It might be flies or something buzzing around the bait spilled outside of the barrel. I slowly reach over and pick up Dad's binoculars, which are sitting between us. I turn the dial to focus in on the bait. With both hands on the binos, I have to raise my heels to keep my gun from sliding off my lap.

With the help of the binoculars, I can see every detail. There are a million bees and flies. Suddenly, I catch movement in the barrel itself. Out pops a red squirrel with a puffy tail and beady black eyes. The bees don't seem to bother him one bit as he scoots by with a mouthful of bread. Birds keep swooping in too to grab a bite. They land, poke, pick, and then race off.

It's all very cool. It's like watching a mini world in action. Each creature appears to be going about its mission with persistence.

I pull the binos away and look at the barrel with my naked eyes. It's funny—now I can't really see anything happening over there. Without being able to zoom in with the binos, I wouldn't have any clue about all that action. I'm so glad Dad always brings his binoculars when we hunt. I'm amazed at what you can see with them.

"Take a look at the bait," I whisper as I slowly hand the binos to Dad.

Moving in slow motion, Dad takes the binos and holds them up to his eyes. He points them at the barrel for a while, then scans around in the woods. As he sets the binoculars back down between us, he gives me a smile and a nod.

"We're feeding a lot of mouths with that bait," he whispers in my ear, leaning over. "Some big, some small."

I carefully analyze the area around the barrel. I notice two beat-down trails that come from the woods and end at the barrel.

The trails are pretty good sized—a bear must have made them. It's a good sign.

Suddenly, I hear a twig break. My heart skips a beat, and heat instantly pours over my body. I turn to Dad with wide eyes, waiting for his confirmation.

He slowly nods. Without raising his hand, he points his finger to the right of the barrel. Like turning the periscope of a submarine, I ease my head around slowly. I focus on the spot in the thick brush and squeeze my gun tight in my lap.

Then, another crack. This time, it's even closer. It's definitely an animal, and it's coming to the barrel.

Catching movement, I lock in. With all my senses hyperfocused on the spot, I see glimpses of black moving through the thick green forest. And then the figure finally pops out from the brush. To my surprise, it's only a giant porcupine!

I look at Dad with disgust and let out the long breath of air I've been holding in.

He just smiles. I get the feeling he knew it wasn't a bear all along.

Mr. Porky marches right in as if he owned the place. All the bees, flies, and birds scatter when he stands in the middle of the bait. I pick up the binoculars again so I can get a close-up.

He may not be a bear, but Mr. Porky is super cool with his giant quills and little black eyes. He doesn't waste any time before chowing down. Eventually, the bees and flies settle back in.

The red squirrel peeks around the barrel at the porcupine, then jumps on top of the barrel and darts back and forth. The red little dude definitely has a problem with the new arrival. When the squirrel finally gets the courage to sneak in and nab another chunk of bread, Mr. Porky gives him a look but doesn't react.

I set the binoculars down and settle back in my seat. I wonder what time it is, so I slide my phone out of my pocket. To my surprise, we've been sitting for two hours. Prime-time bear hunting is getting close.

When the sun settles below the trees and the cool evening air fills the woods, bears like to get moving. And I am ready for some bear action.

But then my thoughts vanish in a flash when Dad taps my left leg. I look up—two black bear cubs about the size of five-gallon buckets are standing on one of the trails. One is standing up, looking at the porcupine, clearly confused about what to do.

Suddenly, a giant bear appears behind the cubs. My eyes pop wide open when I see the enormous mass of black muscle in its chest and legs. I can feel my heart gaining speed. The bear slowly stands up on its massive hind legs and looks over the cubs to see what's holding things up. The bear is so tall, I know it would be looking down on Dad if he were standing next to it.

But what I don't know is whether it's a boar (a male) or a sow (a female). If it's a sow, it's likely the cub's mom. We can't— and wouldn't even want to—shoot her. So for now, all I can do is wait for the bear to reveal itself. My grip on my gun tightens even more.

Quicker than I ever knew a porcupine could move, Mr. Porky is out of there. The standing cub must feel pretty tough, figuring she's the one who caused his retreat. With the coast clear, the first cub marches in and gets right down to eating business.

The giant bear stays back a few yards and seems to be monitoring the situation. Just then, the second cub comes lumbering in and tackles the first cub without warning. The two roll around, pop up, and then race back to the barrel.

My heart rate finally slows down when I realize the big bear is indeed the cubs' mom. She's by far the biggest bear I've ever seen, though. She finally waddles her way in and lays down at the edge of the bait. With her giant paw, she pulls piles of food toward her and starts chowing down.

Nearby, the cubs continue to play. This is amazing! They're extremely cute. These must be the cubs we saw in the trail camera photos. But I've never seen cubs in live action like this before.

I look over at Dad and mouth the words "So cool!"

He gives me a thumbs-up from his lap.

We watch for the rest of the night as the mom devours the bait and the cubs eat, play, and romp around. I sneak my phone out to get some great video and a few pictures.

As the light in the woods starts to fade, I remind myself to stay hopeful. Maybe a big boar will come out and give me a chance.

Just then, a gunshot rings out. My heart jumps. Dad and I quickly look at each other.

"Megan," Dad says just loud enough for me to hear.

I smile and nod, hoping it's true.

The bears are clearly not affected by the shot. They still go about their business as if nothing had happened. Only ten minutes later, I realize I can hardly make out their outlines. The light is nearly gone now.

All of a sudden, the moaning howl of a timber wolf fills the air. It doesn't seem that far away. A second wolf responds way off in the distance. Moments later, the first wolf howls again. It's even closer this time.

Dad and I look over our shoulders to the trail. I can see a dark spot moving toward us. Even momma bear stands up to take notice. I hear panting, then I see a magnificent gray-and-black wolf.

It stops, raises its head to the sky, and cries out a spooky, deep, moaning howl. The sound overpowers the peaceful evening air and sends chills down my back. As soon as the howl ends, the wolf bolts into the woods directly away from us, as if it were on a mission.

"Wow! That was crazy," I can hear Dad say under his breath. I'm not sure if he's talking to me or himself.

I just nod my head in disbelief.

Dad leans over and whispers, "This will be interesting, but we have to get going."

I gulp. I almost forgot we have to climb down from the stand and walk back to the four-wheeler—with a protective momma bear only twenty-five steps away and a timber wolf out there somewhere!

"Let's ease down and hope the bears either stay there or run away. We don't want anything to do with that mom," Dad says. He slips his headlamp band around his forehead, and I do the same.

Dad climbs down first with my gun. I keep an eye on the bears. As best as I can see through the darkness, they're still eating away.

Now it's my turn. I quickly slide down the ladder. This is wild! I sure am glad to have Dad with me at this moment. I have all the confidence in the world that he will keep us safe.

When I hit the ground, we don't waste any time getting out of there. We turn on our headlamps. The white light fills the trail and gives me a little sense of control. It's always spooky when you can't see what's in the woods around you, especially when you just left a giant momma bear with two cubs. I keep peeking behind us, making sure we aren't being followed. The timber wolves howl off in the distance—it doesn't make the walk out any more fun.

We make it to the four-wheeler, jump on, start it up, and race out of there.

"That was interesting!" Dad says, turning his head back toward me so I can hear him over the buzzing of the motor.

"That's for sure! I won't forget this evening anytime soon," I reply.

I smile to myself. It was an exciting night, even though I didn't get a shot off. But I sure hope Megan did—and I can't wait to find out how her night went.

Chapter 8

We roll through the open garage door. The engine echoes as we come to a halt. There's no sign of Megan or Greg. I check my phone. Sure enough, there's a text from Greg. I quickly read it, my eyes getting big.

"Greg says Megan shot a giant and needs our help!" I relay to Dad.

"Wonderful! Let's hook up the trailer and drive out there."

Dad pulls the four-wheeler back outside and drives up to the little black trailer. I hand Dad my cased gun, then I shove the trailer hitch onto the ball and latch it tight. I jump back on and grab my gun.

"Let's roll!" I shout.

I'm fired up. I can't wait to see Megan's bear. I can tell Dad's excited too because he's racing down the trail. I have to hold on for dear life, and the trailer bounces behind us.

We fly past Greg's parked four-wheeler and drive right up to the final trail leading to their stand. Dad kills the engine, and we wait for the sound to settle. We turn on our headlamps and glance out toward the barrel, looking for Greg and Megan. Chances are, they're out there somewhere, next to where the bear dropped.

Then we hear a whistle.

"Up here," Greg says from above.

In confusion, both Dad and I look up and shine our lights in the direction of the sound. Greg and Megan are still sitting in their stand. They shine a flashlight back down at us.

"What are you doing up there?" Dad asks.

"Sure seems like a nice night to sit in a stand and gaze at the stars," Greg says.

"We're too scared to get down!" Megan confesses.

"Oh yah—maybe that's why we're still here," Greg admits too.

Dad and I both break out laughing. We can see Greg smiling in the stand.

"Seriously, though," Greg says, "that thing is giant. Why don't we stay up here while you guys go find him?"

Dad shakes his head with a big grin, clearly getting a kick out of this whole situation. "Did it seem like a good shot?" he asks.

"Looked perfect. But he still took off like a rocket," Greg says.

"Where?" Dad asks.

Greg points his flashlight into the woods. "Right over there."

Even with all our lights shining in that direction, we can't see any trace of the bear—dead or alive. Greg is certain Megan's shot was on the mark. Odds are, the bear only made it a little way into the woods before it dropped. But just the idea of Dad going into the woods to investigate sends shivers down my spine.

"Okay, Luke—you better give me your shotgun for this little adventure," Dad says. "I'm not going in without a gun."

I quickly hand him my gun. "I'm not very excited about going in without one, but I'll back you," I say.

I hand Dad three shells. Like an expert, he has the gun loaded in record time. He'll keep the safety on, but I'm sure his finger will be right on it.

"Let's go find this bear," Dad says, raising his eyebrows with a little craziness in his eyes.

I follow Dad over to the barrel, each step a little tenser than the last. We scan the ground with our headlamps, looking for blood. Still in the stand, Greg calls out directions, guiding us around until we find the first specks of bright-red blood. The small drops quickly turn into big drips.

"This is a nice blood trail," Dad says confidently. "He's hit good."

"That's for sure," I agree.

With our heads down like bloodhounds, we follow the red spots for about fifteen steps, then it leads to a thicket. The bear clearly went in, but it looks like he left us a tunnel rather than a trail.

"This will be interesting!" Dad gives me the same look he gave me when we went through the haunted house at the state fair. "Here we go."

Dad gets down on his hands and knees and lets the gun and the light lead the way into the thicket.

"Be careful!" comes Megan's muffled plea. I can tell she has her hands covering her face.

I stay right behind Dad and do my best not to take a branch in the face. We're only a few crawls in when I hear Dad say, "Hold tight."

I peek over his shoulder. There's a black blob just in front of us. My wide eyes focus on the fur, trying to sense whether there's the slightest movement.

"I sure hope he's dead," I say.

"Me too . . ." comes slowly from Dad.

After a couple of intense moments, Dad eases the gun forward and pokes the barrel into the thick black fur. There's no movement whatsoever.

"Whew! He's done," Dad proclaims.

I let out the long breath I was clearly holding without realizing it.

"Okay, we found him!" Dad yells. "You guys can come down and get him out of here!"

"Whoo-hoo!" Megan howls.

Dad unloads my gun and hands it back to me. "Why don't you go set this down, then come back and help me with this big fella."

I crawl out of the thicket and lay the gun against an old pine tree, then crawl back in. Dad and I grab onto the rear legs and start dragging the giant bear to open ground. We can move him only about a foot with each pull. This bear is huge and heavy!

Megan comes running over to check out her bear. "Oh my goodness! He's bigger than I thought!" she says. She carefully rubs her left hand through the thick black fur.

"Oh, look who decided it was okay to finally get down!" Dad jokes as Greg finally makes his way to us.

Greg responds by pretending to take charge of the situation, as if he were the brave one. "You guys okay? Everybody cool?" he asks with a classic Greg smile.

"Yes, everything's good now. I'm just glad we could be of service to you," Dad shoots back.

"I knew you and Luke would know just how to handle this whole situation," Greg says.

We all kneel around the bear as our lights circle him. Each of us run our hands through the pure black fur that's amazingly thick and coarse.

This is it—all our hard work paid off. Megan finally got her first bear. And what an awesome first bear!

"Well, Megan, this sure looks like the big guy from the pictures. How does it feel to get him?" Dad asks.

She shakes her head, her eyes wide. "I can't begin to explain how I'm feeling. I'm so excited that I finally got a bear. But I'm also a little sad that I took this amazing animal." She pauses. "I have never felt anything like this."

Dad nods knowingly. "Hunting can have mixed emotions," he tells her. "Just know that you did a good thing. We have too many bears in our area. Hunting is one of the only ways we can control the population. Also, you will honor this bear by enjoying and sharing the awesome meat. Not to mention, I'm guessing your dad will probably have a rug made out of this thick fur, and then we can all enjoy him for years to come."

"I'm really proud of you, Megan," Greg says. "You kept your cool, and you made a great shot. And this bear will fill our freezers to the top. Matter of fact, I can almost taste—right now—the maple sausage we'll have made up!"

"Speaking of food," Dad says, "let's get this guy cleaned up and head back so we can have some dinner. I'm starving."

"Hold your horses!" Greg bellows. "We first need to take some pictures."

Of course, Dad is happy to take a bunch of pictures. First of Megan and the bear, then Megan and Greg with the bear, and then all of us in a selfie. Pictures are Dad's thing. He's very good at capturing the memories of the animals that are taken.

After heaving the bear into the trailer, we take off. I bounce on the back of the four-wheeler, and we head for the cabin. I can't stop thinking about how cool it is for Megan to have bagged that bear. But now I'm even more excited to get one myself.

A jolt of energy shoots through my body as I picture a bear like Megan's walking in to our bait. I remember those huge tracks we saw earlier near our stand. I sure hope Big Bear Feet is another giant male and not the one Megan just got.

But then I remember we're supposed to head back home tomorrow afternoon. That means we won't have another chance to hunt.

I have to convince Dad to change the plan and let us stay and hunt. I have to get back in the stand.

I have to make this happen!

Chapter 9

The next morning, I wake up to the amazing smell of bacon. When I pull my head outside my sleeping bag, there's plenty of light filling the bunk room. I glance at the little black alarm clock in the corner. When the red numbers come into focus, they read 9:27.

I roll out of the top bunk and slide down to the floor. I glance out the window to see the sun shining and a bright-blue sky. It's the perfect day. There's even a doe eating clover in field. I throw my clothes on and follow my nose down to the kitchen.

"Smells good down here," I say, my voice a little groggy.

"Hey there," Greg says. "If it isn't guide number two. Pull up a chair next to guide number one."

I take a seat at the table next to Dad. Immediately, I start thinking about when—and how—to ask him if we can stay longer to get one last chance at a bear tonight. But then Greg brings me a plate with two giant steaming pancakes and three slices of mouthwatering bacon.

"I figure the least I can do is cook you guys breakfast for all your hard work last night," he says, patting us on the back.

Now all I can think about is food! After loading up on butter and syrup, I dive in. The breakfast fills me right up.

We then spend the day four-wheeling, shooting some clay pigeons with our shotguns, and splitting some wood for future bonfires. Around three o'clock, Greg and Megan start loading their car.

"Hey, are you guys heading home?" I ask Megan.

She shrugs. "I guess. That's what my dad said. I heard him and your dad talking about wanting to get home for dinner."

Panic instantly sets in. I had so much fun today, I forgot to talk to Dad about staying for the evening! But there's no way I'm ready to go home, so I have to go work some magic.

I scoot to the garage, where I find Dad sweeping for the second time of the day.

"So . . ." I begin. "What's our plan for this evening?"

Dad glances at me from the corner of his eye but keeps sweeping. "I thought we'd just finish cleaning up here and then head out. You've got school tomorrow, you know."

"Are you kidding?" I exclaim, unable to hold it any longer. "We can't go home yet! I have to sit in the stand tonight and give it one more chance! I'm begging you, Dad. My homework's done. And I'll even clean the cabin and do the dishes, if that's what it takes."

Dad stops sweeping. He leans over the broom with his two cupped hands holding him up.

"Mmm," comes out through a slow, deep breath. "It sounds like someone is pretty determined to hunt."

"I am! You and Grandpa always said that the more time you put in the stand, the better your chances. Right?"

"Oh, now you're bringing Grandpa into this. You're a funny guy," Dad says, shaking his head slowly. He sizes me up with a small smirk. "Well, mister, for starters, I'll take you up on the offer to clean the cabin. But first you have to call your mother and see if you can convince her to let us stay. You know she isn't happy when I get you home late on a school night. This is all you, buddy."

"I'll call Mom right now!" I quickly shoot back, sensing a victory. "I can sweet-talk her into one more hunt. I know I can. She loves it when we hunt together!"

"Good luck. Let me know how it goes," Dad says, getting back to sweeping.

When I call Mom, she does some serious drilling about whether my homework is done and whether I have any big tests at school tomorrow. Then she finally gives in and lets us stay for the evening hunt. I'm lucky she's a softy when it comes to Dad spending time with us kids hunting or fishing. The important thing is, I did it—I made another hunt happen! I'm pumped.

A short while later, Greg and Megan finish loading and are ready to head back home. We do some high fives and more congratulating, then we watch them ramble through the gate and onto the dirt road. After hearing two toots of his horn, we give one last wave, then head back inside.

I promised Dad I would clean the cabin, so I get right to work. It takes me longer than I thought to vacuum, sweep, and wash the dishes. Before I know it, the microwave clock says it's 4:22. I take one last look around, feeling satisfied with my job. Then I run out to the garage, where Dad has been busy cleaning up.

"We have to get moving!" I say, standing half in the doorway.

Dad looks at his watch. "Holy cow— you're right. Are you done inside?"

"It's spotless," I say proudly.

We throw on our hunting clothes, lace up our boots, and head out the door, all in about ten minutes. I'm filled with anticipation as the four-wheeler bounces down the familiar trail.

Once we park in our spot, I uncase my trusty 20-gauge and slide three slugs in. Dad tosses the backpack over his shoulder. Without a word, we march on our way to the stand.

We don't get ten steps from the four-wheeler when Dad says, "Look at that."

In a puddle that still holds some water is a perfect bear track.

"That's new. It looks like it's Big Bear Feet again," Dad says. "If the shoe fits, wear it. And in his case, he would need a really big shoe," Dad adds with a smile.

I just shake my head and play along. He's right, though—the bear would need a big shoe! I smile with excitement, realizing that this new track is proof that it didn't come from the bear Megan got last night.

I'm filled with new energy and hope we'll see him tonight.

We continue down the trail. At about the halfway mark, I hear a twig crack to my right. I quickly look over. Way closer than I expect is one of the cubs.

Catching me off guard, Dad pulls me back with one arm. He keeps me close as I regain my balance. At the same time, the little dude scoots off running.

"Stay still, hold tight," Dad whispers in my ear. "There's the mom and the other cub right there. We don't want to give her any reason to think we're putting her cub in danger."

Sure enough, the mom and other cub are only about fifteen steps away. They have no idea we're here. But when the other cub comes running, the mom instantly turns and bolts out of sight with the two cubs stuck right behind her. In a flash, they're gone.

Dad pulls me in tighter with his one arm. "Whew! That could have been interesting."

"You're not kidding," I say, my heart still beating like mad.

"Let's get to the stand before we get eaten," Dad says with a nod and a wink.

Like soldiers making our way through enemy territory, we stay on full alert the whole way to our stand. When we finally settle in high above ground, I let out a quick breath of relief. This bear hunting stuff can be a little spooky at times.

"After our little encounter, I don't think we'll be seeing momma bear and the cubs again tonight," Dad whispers.

"That's fine," I say optimistically. "I'm hoping we see Big Bear Feet, anyway!"

Chapter 10

It's the perfect fall afternoon. A slight breeze causes the leaves to dance and shimmer through the sun. The wind is in our face, which helps keep our scent away from the bait. The light jacket I'm wearing is almost too warm, but I keep it on. I know it will cool down as the sun settles.

The stage is set for a wonderful show. Through Dad's binoculars, I once again see the dancing bees and flies enjoying the sweet Peeps and sugary treats scattered around the barrel. The red squirrel still seems overflowing with energy or nervousness as it races in and out. Overhead, a flock of crows circle and caw, clearly disappointed we've invaded the area. A group of little chickadees pop on the ground around us, in the bushes, and in the trees. Two even land on the branch next to us, give us a look-over, and then bolt on their way.

I settle back into my seat and make myself comfortable. We most likely have a while yet until any bears would come out. I try to keep a watch out, but my mind starts to drift away. I imagine I'm an intergalactic hero flying a spaceship . . .

Suddenly, I hear a twig crack. That's when I realize my eyes are closed. It seems my spaceship daydream had turned into a real dream. I must have dozed off!

Opening my eyes as wide as they will go, I try to snap back into reality. I quickly assess the location of the sun. I'm relieved to see it isn't much lower than before I drifted off. I haven't been snoozing for long.

A twig snaps again, and I glance over at Dad. He smiles and nods in the direction of the sound. My eyes pierce through the thick green undergrowth in search of the twig breaker. Out comes Mr. Porky without a worry in the world.

I watch him munch on the treats for a bit, but then the sun drops and hits us right in the eyes. This stand is a little tricky because it faces straight west. As the sun goes down each evening, we have about thirty minutes of it shining directly behind the barrel. When it's cloudy, as it was last night, it's not so bad. But tonight, I have to squint and look away from the piercing rays to protect myself from going blind. I try to glance from the corner of my eyes just to make sure nothing new is happening at the bait.

Finally, the sun falls like a deflated balloon below the trees. The last glow of the evening's light fills the woods with a calm purple-gray. I look up and see a pure white streak left over from a passing plane. It cuts through the sky like a perfect paint stroke. I take a deep, long breath and smile. There is just something magical about sitting in a stand on a perfect day. I'm a lucky kid, getting to do this with my dad—and I know it.

I feel a tap on my left leg. Dad's pointing to Mr. Porky. I glance over and then cock my head to study the porcupine's strange stance. His back is arched way up high. It looks as if he's trying to stretch out or do yoga or something. Dad and I both shrug, clearly confused as to what Mr. Porky is doing.

Seemingly out of nowhere, a giant bear suddenly jumps out of the woods and roars. In shock, I gasp out loud and reel back in the stand. My shoulders jam against the railing—I can't retreat any farther without falling out. Even Dad seems to prepare for impact. He has his hands stretched out and his feet up, all to protect himself.

Before I can even take my next breath, Mr. Porky is gone, and the bear is looking in the barrel. With no cubs in sight, it's definitely a boar. And he's huge. He sniffs the air around the barrel and swoops down with his huge open jaws. Wasting no time, he takes a giant mouthful of oil-soaked bread.

This is it. It's go time. My heart pounds as I reach for my trusty 20-gauge. My whole body seems to be trembling, but I still manage to lift my gun off my lap.

With his right hand, Dad squeezes my knee firmly, and with his left, he pads the air calmly. Without sound, he mouths, "Relax . . . breathe."

Is he *crazy*? I've been waiting for this moment for a long time. After all the work we've done, and after all the hours of sitting in the stand, it's finally happening. The bear of my dreams just appeared with a grand entrance that not only scared Mr. Porky half to death but also made Dad and me nearly jump out of the stand. There's no calming down! The adrenaline will race through my veins until I get this bear.

Then again, I *do* need to stay calm enough to make a good shot. He's standing broadside to us—the perfect angle. As long as I'm steady, this shot will be a slam dunk, thanks to all the target-practicing I have done. I take a long, deep breath and slowly let it out. It works—I feel a slight calm in my chest.

But just as I ease my gun up to my shoulder, the bear raises his nose up into the air. A new smell has caught his attention—our smell! The breeze has shifted. I can feel it hitting the back of my neck, which means it's pushing our scent right toward the bear.

The giant boar turns his head back and forth, trying to pinpoint the source of the new smell. Then he looks right at us, just as if I had shouted out, "Here we are, bear!" He's caught our scent. I know it instantly.

He stands up and faces our direction. No shot. I need him to turn sideways again.

The perfect shot is right behind his shoulder, where his heart and lungs are. With my gun up and lightning shooting through my body, I hold as steady as I can. I must wait out this stare-down.

I get the feeling the bear is ready to bolt out of there. Sure enough, he drops back to his feet, turns, and takes two quick steps toward the safety of the thick woods.

But then he stops, turns broadside, and gives us one last look.

"Take him," I hear Dad say.

Without hesitation, I aim and pull the trigger. BOOM! the gun barks out. It kicks me back, and a small poof of white smoke rises from the barrel.

"You got him!" Dad yells before I can fix my eyes back on the bear.

I instantly pump another shell in the chamber, ready for another shot.

"You don't need that—he's down right there," Dad says.

I look out. The bear had dropped in his tracks and is now lying motionless.

"Great shot! Way to go, buddy!" Dad just about knocks me out of the stand as he slaps me on the back. "How cool was that?"

"Wow," is all I can muster.

I put the safety back on and hand the gun to Dad. As I sit back in the stand, I can feel my whole body shake. I take a big, deep breath and let it out fast, trying to clear my nerves. Still in shock, I stare at the pure black mass lying out there.

I cannot believe what just happened and how quickly things can change. One minute I'm napping, then I'm looking at a porcupine, and then moments later I'm staring down the barrel at a giant black bear. That's hunting—you never know what you're going to get.

I turn to Dad and give him a crushing high five. "Let's go check him out!"

We make our way to the bear, busting through the brush a little faster than normal. Even though we're confident he's done, I poke him with my gun barrel to be absolutely sure. Then I unload my gun and prop it up against a tree.

I go to the bear, drop to my knees, and run my hands through his thick black fur. He's amazing—everything I dreamed a bear to be.

Dad picks up a front paw and compares it to his own outstretched hand.

"That's one big bear paw," Dad says, shaking his head.

"Nope—that's Big Bear Feet!" I say with a proud smile.

It's time for pictures, and we take a bunch. Then we go to work getting the bear ready to drop off at the butcher's.

When we finally get home, it's a little later than Mom had wanted, but she's all smiles when I walk through the door. She knows how cool it is for us to get animals—especially my first bear.

In the end, my persistence paid off. It was one of the best weekends ever!

About the Author

Kevin Lovegreen was born, raised, and lives in Minnesota with his loving wife and two amazing children. Hunting, fishing, and the outdoors have always been a big part of his life. From chasing squirrels as a child to chasing elk as an adult, Kevin loves the thrill of hunting. But even more, he loves telling the stories of the adventure. Presenting at schools and connecting with kids about the outdoors is one of his favorite things to do.

Monster Mule Deer

Lucky Luke's
25lb. turkey

The
Muddy
Elk

Crysta
1st bu

Lucky Luke
with a larg
mouth bass

Lucky Luke's
1st bear

Crystal, The Swamp hero!

www.KevinLovegreen.com

Other books in the series

To order books, sign up for book alerts, or to
see great pictures visit:

www.KevinLovegreen.com

All the stories in the Lucky Luke's Hunting Adventures series are based on real experiences that happened to me or my family.

If you like the book, please help spread the word by telling all your friends!

Thanks for reading!
Kevin Lovegreen